Ethics and Infinity

EMMANUEL LEVINAS

ETHICS AND INFINITY

Conversations with Philippe Nemo
Translated by Richard A. Cohen

Duquesne University Press
Pittsburgh

First published in French
under the title *Ethique et infini*
© *Librairie Arthème Fayard et Radio France, 1982*

English translation copyright
© *1985 by Duquesne University Press*
All Rights Reserved
Manufactured in the United States of America

*Published in the United States of America
by Duquesne University Press
600 Forbes Avenue, Pittsburgh, PA 15282*

Library of Congress Cataloging in Publication Data

*Levinas, Emmanuel.
Ethics and Infinity.
Translation of: Ethique et infini
Bibliography: p.
1. Philosophy—Addresses, essays, lectures.
I. Title.
B29.L48513   1985   194   85-1542
ISBN 0-8207-0178-5*

Contents

 *Interviewer's Preface*

THE interviews presented in this volume were recorded and broadcast by Radio France-Culture in February-March 1981. They have been slightly recast and finished for publication. They constitute a succinct presentation of the philosophy of Emmanuel Levinas, the whole of which could without doubt conform to the title *Ethics and Infinity*. The ten interviews follow the development of Levinas' thought since his student days up to the most recent articles, dedicated to the question of God — articles which came to be put together into a collection[1] — proceeding through two short but important works, *Existence and Existents* and *Time and the Other*, and the two major philosophical works, *Totality and Infinity* and *Otherwise than Being or Beyond Essence*.

Though succinct — a number of aspects of

1. *De Dieu qui vient a l'idée* (Paris: J. Vrin, 1982)

Levinas' philosophy are not broached — this presentation is nevertheless faithful, in a special sense. It is in fact formulated by the author himself, taking a general point of view of his work, agreeing to simplify the expression of his arguments, not taking refuge behind his own reputation and the list of his complete works — thus taking a course counter to the falseness and unreasonableness customary in our academies. It is thus faithful to that faithfulness which assures to a discourse the living presence of its author.

Commenting on Plato's *Phædrus*, Levinas has often himself insisted on this sovereignty and modesty of the author, father of the discourse, orally defending the written discourse which one challenges and misunderstands, putting it back into play and submitting it to the test of the instant, of the actually present other person for whom it is finally destined. In this sense, and in this situation, the *saying* of the living author authenticates the *said* of the deposited work, because it alone can resay the said, and thus heighten its truth. The author, speaking of his thought, decides what he wants to resay. What he at times yields to the exigencies of the interlocutor vindicates with so much the more clearness that to which he holds above all. Such is the exercise Levinas agreed to give himself up to in answering our questions. It is true that these did not urge him to express himself on themes other than those he had treated at great length in his books — which does not exclude new developments and illuminations.

Emmanuel Levinas is the philosopher of ethics, without doubt the sole moralist of contemporary thought. But to those who believe him a specialist in ethics as if ethics were a specialty, these few pages, before the reading of his works, teach his essential thesis: that ethics if first philosophy, starting from which the other branches of metaphysics take their meaning. For the first question, that by which being is torn and the human established as "otherwise than being" and transcendence in the world, that without which, in return, any other interrogation of thought is no more than vanity and chasing the wind — is the question of justice.

Ph.N.

Emmanuel Levinas was born in January, 1906, in Kaunas, Lithuania. Secondary studies in Lithuania and Russia. Philosophy studies in Strasbourg from 1923 to 1930. Stay in Fribourg in 1928-1929 close to Husserl and Heidegger. Naturalized French in 1930. Professor of philosophy, director of the Oriental Isrælite Normal School. Professor of philosophy at the University of Poitiers (1964), of Paris-Nanterre (1967), then at the Sorbonne (1973).[1]

1. On Levinas, cf. Emmanuel Levinas, "Signature," edited by Adrian Peperzak, transl. by Mary Ellen Petrisko, *Research in Phenomenology*, Vol. VIII, 1978, pp. 175-189. [Tr. note]

INTERVIEWER'S PREFACE

Philippe Nemo was born in 1949. He is considered one of France's "new philosophes," a group of thinkers disillusioned with their Marxism in the face of the events of May 1968. He is author of *L'Homme Structural* and *Job et l'Excès du Mal*. [Tr. note]

Translator's Introduction

Better Than Being

THE critique of metaphysics in our day has not been a simple revival of the Voltairean attack on provincialism and superstition. Grown more wary, it is an attack on the surface as well as the soul of Western metaphysics. Heidegger has taught us to grasp and think through the subtle metaphysics which hides in language, in its formal, representational, foundational, willful and subjectivist tendencies.

Heidegger has taught that the history of Western thought and culture since its Greek beginnings has been an "onto-theo-logy": theology in the guise of ontology. What is truly present is not the manifest unfolding of what is, but a being with more being than the passing show of existence. This preeminent being — idea, energeia, substance, position, concept, dialectic, will to power, will to will — serves as the paradigm, the model, the foundation for what being its poorer relations — beings — might have. The world is but the reflection, the re-presentation of God, substance, transcendental ego, etc.. The world, then, is already a secondary text, and philosophy is a commentary on commentary.

Against onto-theo-logy, in contrast, Heidegger reintroduces the world to thought. He reintroduces a thinking of the world, of this world in its coming to be and its passing away, the "worlding of the world," its historical revelation. Heidegger proposes the difficult task of thinking without recourse to metaphysics, teasing language from its metaphysical wiles. He has sought a language in which be-ing can speak, a language free of the deceptive logic of identity and presence, of the forcing and manhandling constitutive of metaphysics.

What role is assigned to ethics in such a thought? While Heidegger claims his own task is neither to support nor to oppose this or that worldly morality, it becomes clear that with the end of traditional philosophy, the task of genuine thinking is itself an ethics. What becomes most needful is a responsibility for the world, a caring for what is as it is, a shepherding, a letting be, an allowance for being's generosity, an attunement to the gift giving of worlds. Ontology becomes indebtedness to what is, a quiet listening vigilant against its own interference, cautious of its own interventions, careful not to disturb. In a word, thinking becomes a lovingkindness.

But is not ethics by nature metaphysical? Does

it not depend on the essentially metaphysical distinction between "what is" and "what ought to be"? Is not ethics then equivalent to onto-theo-logy, to the sanctions a being can hold over beings?

For Nietzsche, like Heidegger, the era of metaphysics — the history of a long error — the moralization of being, the hubris of unbounded subjectivism, is over, exposed, unmasked in its deceptive presumption. A new age and a new humanity are called for, an age of honesty, courage and innocence. Henceforth existence will be affirmed joyously, gaily, in its coming to be and its passing away, in its expenditure without reserve, its bountifulness. Henceforth our obligations will be our own, authentic, in the self-conscious creation of value or the quiet harkening to being.

And yet Levinas insists on ethics, on a metaphysical responsibility, an exorbitant and infinite responsibility for other human beings, to care not for being, for the unravelling of its plot, but for what is beyond and against being, the alterity of the other person. "Do I have," he asks, "the *right* to be?"

Has Levinas misunderstood the critique of metaphysics? Is his yet another, perhaps subtler, return to slave morality, a fall into an ontics forgetful of being, weighed down by the spirit of gravity? What, we must ask again, *is* the status of ethics in a post-metaphysical age? It is Levinas' unique place to suggest, no, to insist, that ethics only comes into its own with the collapse of onto-theo-logy.

For Levinas the critique of metaphysics indeed ends onto-theo-logical ethics, the ethics of transcendent sanction, of other worldly principles and rules. Yet in the *correctness* of the critique of metaphysics he discerns another alternative than the joyous dance of existence, the poetic language of being, or the playful games of language. He discerns that with this critique we can now recognize that all along ontology, whether onto-theo-logical or not, has been the wrong standard for ethics, that it is an *inferior* standard. Ethics not only survives the end of metaphysics, it finally comes into its own with the end of metaphysics. How is this so?

Here again, cautions must be taken. Heidegger has taught us the care for language. The real difficulty with questioning — which is philosophy's task — lies in the questions themselves, in the places they take us unawares. Presupposed in the question of the status of ethics is the question of just what ethics is. What is ethics? Are moralities essentially onto-theological, as Heidegger and Nietzsche seem to say, or do they manifest something else, something quite different, with different structures and demands, with a different relation to manifestation itself? Taking up Heidegger's care for language, but now oddly against him, as we shall see, we must uncover the metaphysical intrigues of language to escape misunderstanding the status of ethics in a post-metaphysical age.

Heidegger's question seems the most philosophical of questions: "What is . . .?" What is thinking? What is poetry? What is technology? And now, what is ethics? If in this question we can uncover an onto-theo-logical bent, then we are on the way to grasping its inappropriateness with regard to ethics, if indeed ethics survives the end of metaphysics. Perhaps, by doing this, the mystery and strangeness which surrounds the later writings of Heidegger, the peculiar meanderings of his path out of metaphysics can be grasped in an entirely new way. Is the very question of essence, the "What is . . .?" question, itself too metaphysically compromised?

The mind rebels. What could be more *essential* to any sort of intelligent inquiry, to any sort of thinking, than to ask what something *is*, to seek its essence, to know it as it is, in its manifestation? What is more unavoidable than asking *what ethics is* to discover if ethics is onto-theo-logical and hence metaphysical in the corrupting sense?

Since Socrates thought has been intimately tied to the cautions which inhere in the question of essence. We insist on asking and knowing what something is before committing ourselves to action or belief. Indeed, such caution has become our very action, our reserve and wariness. Knowledge of the essence, essential knowledge, precedes the existential: Socrates thought before he acted, he pauses before the symposium, to contemplate, to deliberate, to ask what's what. "To know the good," he taught, "is to do the good"; so tied were thinking and human being. Socrates defeated the "ignorance" of opponent after opponent with his questioning. His interlocutors learned that they must *first* know the good in order to *then* do it, that they must be philosophers, lovers of wisdom before all else.

But Nietzsche and Heidegger have made Socrates suspect too. Their suspicions, the inversions they point to, are not, however, what I wish to pursue for the moment. Rather, it is the essentialist form these suspicions still take that is of greater import. We must ask what is the "What is . . .?" question. In Socrates' hands it led to the inversion of consciousness and instincts, the sacrifice of the latter to the former. But what of this question in Heidegger's hands?

Are we not in need of still more precautions? Must we not step back from *this* question to raise another, to recognize the obvious circularity of asking *what is* the "What is . . .?" question? It seems to beg the question. Is our new suspicion, then, that Heidegger begs the question of metaphysics when he asks "What is poetry?" or "What is thinking?"? Yet his thought is insistently anti-metaphysical. Why, then, does he retain the metaphysical question par excellence? Aware of just such an objection, he proposes, against the vicious circle of the *petitio principi*, an alternative, productive circularity: hermeneutic questioning. To ask "What is . . .?" does not partake of onto-theo-logy if one acknowledges (1) that the answer can never be fixed absolutely, but calls essentially, endlessly, for additional "What is . . .?" questions. Dialectical refinement here replaces vicious circularity. Further, beyond the openmindedness called for by dialectical refinement, hermeneutic questioning (2) insists on avoiding subjective impositions, on avoiding reading into rather than harkening to things. One must harken to the things themselves, ultimately to being, in a careful attunement to what is.

But do the refinement and care of the hermeneutic question — which succeed in avoiding onto-theo-logy — succeed in avoiding all viciousness? Certainly they convert a simple fallacy into a productive inquiry, they open a path for thought. But is it not the case that however much refinement and care one brings to bear, to ask what something is leads to asking what something else is, and so on and so forth, *ad infinitum*? What is disturbing in this is not so much the infinity of interpretive depth, which has the virtue of escaping onto-theo-logy and remaining true to the way things are, to the phenomena, the coming to be and passing away of being. Rather, the problem lies in the influence the endlessly open horizon of such thinking exerts on the way of such thought. That is, the problem lies in what seems to be the very virtue of hermeneutic thought, namely, the doggedness of the "What is . . .?" question, in its inability to escape itself, to escape being and essence.

But what could be more inescapable than being and essence? Isn't such a "problem" mere silliness, or return to onto-theo-logy, the craving for a beyond? In what way is the doggedness of essential questioning a constraint, a viciousness? In what way is an

attuned predisposition toward being and essence —
what else could there be? — a flaw?

The only way such questioning can be recognized as problematic is by introducing another sort of
questioning, a questioning structured entirely otherwise, while at the same time structured in a way
which is not itself onto-theo-logical. Such is the ethical question. Rather than asking what ethics is, in the
hope of finding out whether ethics is onto-theo-
logical or not, one can ask if ethics is *better* than being.
This sort of question is not an essential question. It
does not — no matter how respectfully — call for
more vision. The ethical question does not merely
contrast with the question of essence, as if ontological and ethical questions operated on the same
horizon, under the same light; they are not on the
same plane. More-over, the question of essence —
"What is ethics?" — positively and precisely *excludes*
the force of the ethical question. It collapses the
"what ought to be" of ethics into the "what is" of
ontology. I almost said it *obscures* the ethical question,
but the point is that the very standards of obscurity
and clarity are already standards of being and essence. The approach of the ethical question, to the
contrary, is and must be immediately one of moral
height, of obligation and responsibility not for what
is, but for what ought to be. Ethics is not merely
different from thinking, in which case it would eventually be absorbed by thinking's play of differences, it
cuts across ontology, it is radically and irreducibly

"otherwise than being or beyond essence."

The result of the above excursus into the influence of language on questioning seems to be the emergence of two questions rather than one. With the end of onto-theo-logical metaphysics, (1) is ethics still *better*? Does the term "better" still carry *moral* force, divorced from reality claims, from God, substance, transcendental ego, etc.? Or, there remains what appears to be the most philosophical of questions, (2) what is ethics really, if it is anything at all, with the end of onto-theo-logical metaphysics? Depending on which sort of question one asks first, an ethical or an ontological results follows. It seems, then, that the viciousness of question begging has merely been doubled rather than vitiated. Ethical questions yield ethical answers (perhaps). Essential questions yield essential answers.

It is important to see that this is not so, or that if it is so then the "fault" lies with essential questioning. To be, according to Levinas, is not enough, even if such being takes responsibility for the unfolding of being, for the ongoing revelation of worlds. There is a trap in essential questioning, an *ad infinitum* neglectful of its own condition. Ethics, in Levinas' view, occurs "prior" to essence and being, conditioning them. Not, however, because the good is installed in a Heaven above or an identity behind identities, for this would just take the ontological move one step back, would again fall back into onto-theo-logy, once more confusing ethics with ontology, as if what "ought to be" somehow "is." *What* ethics is does not survive the end of metaphysics — but only because ethics never *was* or *is* anything. Ethics does not have an essence, its "essence," so to speak, is precisely not to have an essence, to unsettle essences. Its "identity" is precisely not to have an identity, to undo identities. Its "being" is not to be but to be *better than being*. Ethics is precisely ethics by disturbing the complacency of being (or of non-being, being's correlate). "To be or not to be," Levinas insists, is *not* the question.

Ethics occurs as an an-archy, the compassion of being. Its priority is affirmed without recourse to principles, without vision, in the irrecuperable shock of being-for-the-other-person before being-for-oneself, or being-with-others, or being-in-the-world, to name some of the contemporary philosophical formulas of post-metaphysical thought. Ethical priority, according to Levinas, occurs as the moral height of the other person over being, essence, identity, manifestation, principles, in brief, over me.

There is more to being than being. The surplus of the Other's nonencompassable alterity — not the alterity of horizons — is the way ethics intrudes, disturbs, commands being — from height and destitution. It is the demand made by the very face of the Other in a nakedness which pierces the face which can be objectified. "The face," Levinas says in the pages which follow, "is what one cannot kill, or it is that whose *meaning* consists in saying: 'thou shalt not

—10—

kill.' Murder, it is true, is a banal fact; one can kill the Other; the ethical exigency is not an ontological necessity. The prohibition against killing does not render murder impossible." It renders it evil. One can kill, but it is better not to kill, howevermuch this "better" escapes thematization, representation, formalization, idealization, identification, and all the cautions of essential thinking. To know the good is already not to have done it. One does the good before knowing it — ethics lies in this "before," eternally scandalous to thought.

Neither my consciousness nor my instincts are sufficient to the excessive demand the other places on me. They are cut to the quick. Yet shattered — as shattered, a fission, a "despite-myself," for "no one is good voluntarily," says Levinas — the subject rises to the occasion, subjected to the most passive passivity, saying "Here I am." The crux of ethics lies in the non- encompassable yet non-indifferent relation between the "better" and "being." It is a relation like no other, "a distance which is also proximity," Levinas wrote in 1946, "— which is not a coincidence or a lost union, but signifies all the surplus or all the *goodness* of an original sociality." Responsibility in proximity with the other is "more precious than the fact of being given."[1] It is also more demanding.

As such, the ethical relation escapes thematization. To reduce it to a theme, a principle, a being, an

1. *Le temps et l'autre*, pp. 10-11.

arché, was the mistake of onto-theo-logy. To let being flow in the poetry of language, in its giftgiving, its play, is also to turn from the ethical exigency to the ontological exigency, for being wants only to persevere in being. Ethics *occurs* — to return positively to Socrates — across the hiatus of dialogue, not in the content of discourse, in the continuities or discontinuities of what is said, but in the demand for response. "It is better," Socrates said, "to suffer evil than to do it." Socrates didn't realize that he could not *prove* this point, even though it was in effect while he spoke. The responsibility to respond to the other is, for Levinas, precisely the inordinate responsibility, the infinite responsibility of being-for-the-other *before* oneself — the ethical relation. What is said [*le dit*] can always be unsaid, re-said or revised — it is the *saying* [*le dire*] of it, the intrusion it effects, the interruption it inserts into continuities, as well as the passivity it calls forth, beneath identity, that accomplishes the *priority* and *anteriority* of ethics. The only alterity sufficiently other to provoke response, to subject the subject to the subjection of response — which for Levinas is subjectivity itself, and the meaning of meaning, the event of ethics — is the absolute alterity of the other person encountered in the excessive immediacy of the face-to-face.

Radical alterity figures in Levinas' thought not as a flaw, an ignorance, an obscurity, a childishness, a laziness or a deferral, but as the non-thematizable charge through which ethics commands. "What ought to be" — the subject's response to the Other — relates to "what is" — being, essence, manifestation, phenomenon, identity — not by some subtle or crude conversion into "what is," but by haunting it, disturbing it, raising it to a moral height of which it is not itself capable. The alterity of the other raises the subject in a severe responsibility which bears all the weight of the world's seriousness in a non-indifference — with no ontological basis — for the other.

When in the late 1930s the British colonial administrators asked Gandhi what he expected from his annoying non-violent agitation, the Mahatma replied that he expected the British would quit India. They would quit India *on their own* because they would come to see they were *wrong*. Moral force is a scandal for ontological thinking, whether that thinking is gently attuned to being or imposing its subjective will. The power of ethics is entirely different from the power of identities, whether poetic or political, whether knowledge or administration. It escapes and judges the synthesizing, centralizing forces.

Ethics is forceful not because it opposes power with more power, on the same plane, with a bigger army, more guns, a finer microscope or a grander space program, but rather because it opposes power with what appears to be weakness and vulnerability but is responsibility and sincerity. To the calculations of power, ethics opposes *less* than power can conquer. With their lathi sticks the British occupational police struck their opponents, hurt them dreadfully, but at the same time they were hitting their own injustice, their own inhumanity, and with each blow non-violently received were taught a moral lesson. Not that they were necessarily taught a lesson: ethics is not ontology, it is not necessary, one can kill. Moral force, however, the proximity of the face-to-face, the height and destitution of the other's face, is the ever patient counterbalance to all the powers of the world, including nuclear power. Moral force *is* not stronger than the powers of being and essence, the totalizing, synthesizing powers, it is *better*, and this is its ultimate strength.

Does Levinas' philosophy, then, come down to the escapist lament of slavery, failure, cowardice and inability? Is it a rationalization? "The true problem for us Westerners," he writes in response to just such a question, "is not so much to refuse violence as to question ourselves about a struggle against violence which, without blanching in non-resistance to evil, could avoid the institution of violence out of this very struggle. Does not the war perpetuate that which it is called to make disappear, and consecrate war and its virile virtues in good conscience? One has to reconsider the meaning of a certain human weakness, and no longer see in patience only the reverse side of the ontological finitude of the human. But for that one has to be patient oneself without asking patience of the others — and for that one has to admit a difference between oneself and the others."[2] Only this

2. *Otherwise than being*, p. 177.

difference between oneself and the others, only the individuation which occurs as non-indifference to the plight and height of the other, as ethics, related to and separate from the other, the philosophical scandal of heterogenous experience, is capable — through its very weakness — of holding the march of historical being in check. That is, only ethics can judge — rather than simply appreciate — the epochal unfolding of being.

"But does the subject escape the concept and essence . . . only in resignation and illusion, against which at the hour of truth or of the inevitable awakening, essence is stronger?" Levinas asks. He answers that to grasp the singularity of the subject ethically commanded, one must "understand the subjectivity of the subject *beyond essence*, as on the basis of an *escape* from the concept, a forgetting of being and non-being. Not of an 'unregulated' forgetting . . . but a forgetting that would be an ignorance in the sense that nobility *ignores* what is not noble."[3] Such an ignorance is not blind, it knows too much, more than it can comprehend, more than what can be comprehended — an infinite responsibility before others.

"It is an extremely painful thing," Kafka wrote in his nuanced style, "to be ruled by laws that one does not know."

Richard A. Cohen

3. Ibid..

Translator's Note

DIRECT quotations from Levinas' works have been checked in every instance with their originals and with Lingis' translations when available. Levinas has made some slight, mostly grammatical changes from the originals which, at his request, I have kept intact in the text which follows. I have also made some minor changes in the terminology adopted by Lingis.

I have followed Lingis' convention of always translating *autrui* as the "Other" (with a capital "O") and *autre* as "other" (with a small "o"), regardless of the occasional capitalization of *autre* in the text. *Autrui*, in French, refers to the personal other, the other person; *autre* refers to otherness in general, to alterity.

I would like to thank my colleague André Prévos for his generous help in reviewing the entire translation with me, and my wife Mairi for aiding me in many questions of euphony. The translation is dedicated to my parents Sidney Sheldon Cohen and Bette Gordon Cohen.

One

Bible and Philosophy

Philippe Nemo: How does one begin thinking? Through the questions one poses to and of oneself, following original occurences? Or through the thoughts and works with which one first enters into contact?

Emmanuel Levinas: It probably begins through traumatisms or gropings to which one does not even know how to give a verbal form: a separation, a violent scene, a sudden consciousness of the monotony of time. It is from the reading of books — not necessarily philosophical — that these initial shocks become questions and problems, giving one to think. The role of national literatures is here perhaps very important. Not just that one learns words from it, but in it one lives "the true life which is absent" but which is precisely no longer utopian. I think that in the great fear of bookishness, one underestimates the "ontological" reference of the human to the book that one takes for a source of information, or for a "tool" of learning, a *textbook*, even though it is a *modality* of our being. Indeed, to read is to keep oneself above the realism — or the politics — of our care for ourselves, without coming however to the good intentions of beautiful souls, or to the normative idealism of what "must be." In this sense the Bible would be for me the book par excellence.

Ph.N.: What thus have been for you the first great books encountered, the Bible or the philosophers?

E.L.: Very early the Bible, the first philosophical texts at the university, after a hazy survey of psychology at secondary school and a rapid reading of some pages on "philosophical idealism" in an "Introduction to Philosophy." But between the Bible and the philosophers, the Russian classics — Pushkin, Lermontov, Gogol, Turgenev, Dostoyevsky and Tolstoy, and also the great writers of Western Europe, notably Shakespeare, much admired in *Hamlet*, *Macbeth* and *King Lear*. The philosophical problem understood as the meaning of the human, as the search for the famous "meaning of life" — about which the characters of the Russian novelists ceaselessly wonder — is it a good preparation to Plato and Kant registered in the degree program in philosophy? It takes time to see the transitions.

Ph.N.: How have you harmonized these two modes of thought, the Biblical and philosophical?

E.L.: Were they supposed to harmonize? The religious sentiment such as I had received it consisted much more in respect for books — the Bible and its traditional commentaries going back to the thought of ancient rabbis — than in determinate beliefs. I do not mean by this that it was an attenuated religious sentiment. The sentiment that the Bible is the Book of books wherein the first things are said, those that *became* said so that human life has a meaning, and are said in a form which opens to commentators the same dimension of profundity, was not some simple substitution of a literary judgement onto the consciousness of the "sacred." It is that extraordinary presence of its characters, that ethical plenitude and its mysterious possibilities of exegesis which originally signified transcendence for me. And no less. Hermeneutic glimpsing and feeling, with all their audacity as religious life and liturgy, are of no little importance. The texts of the great philosophers, with the place interpretation holds in their reading, seem to me closer to the Bible than opposed to it, even if the concreteness of Biblical themes was not immediately reflected in the philosophical pages. But I did not have the impression, early on, that philosophy was essentially atheist, and I still do not think it today. And if, in philosophy, verse can no longer take the place of proof, the God of verse can, despite all the text's anthropological metaphors, remain the measure of Spirit for the philosopher.

Ph.N.: One can indeed interpret your subsequent work as an attempt to harmonize the essentials of Biblical theology with the philosophical tradition and its language. For you there must have been more than a peaceful coexistence between the two "libraries"?

E.L.: I have never aimed explicitly to "harmonize" or "conciliate" both traditions. If they happen to be in harmony it is probably because every philosophical thought rests on pre-philosophical experiences, and because for me reading the Bible has belonged to these founding experiences. It has thus played an essential role — and in large part without my knowing it — in addressing all mankind. But what for me measures the religious depth of the Bible's founding experience is also the acute consciousness that the holy Story it tells is not simply a series of finished events, but that it has an immediate actual relation with the fate of the Jewish dispersion in the world. Every intellectual doubt relative to the implicit dogma of this or that other point of this ancient book lost its meaning and effect in what is always serious in real Jewish history. At no moment did the Western philosophical tradition in my eyes lose its right to the last word; everything must, indeed, be expressed in its tongue; but perhaps it is not the place of the first meaning of beings, the place where meaning begins.

Ph.N.: Let's come to that tradition. Who are the first philosophers you read?

E.L.: Even before beginning my studies in philosophy in France, I had read the great Russian writers, as I have said. Serious contact with specifically philosophical literature and with philosophers — was Strasbourg. There, at eighteen, I met four professors to whom, in my spirit, I attach an incomparable prestige: Charles Blondel, Maurice Halbwachs, Maurice Pradines and Henri Carteron.[1] These were

1. Charles Blondel (1876-1939): physician and philosopher; professor of psychology at Strasbourg from 1919 to 1937; author of *La conscience morbide* (1914), *La psychoanalyse* (1924), *La mentalité primitive* (1926), *Introduction à la psychologie collective* (1928), *La psychologie de Marcel Proust* (1932), *La suicide* (1933). Maurice Halbwachs (1877-1945): degrees in mathematics and philosophy; student of Durkheim; author of *La Classe ouvriere et les niveaux de vie* (1913), *Les Cadres sociaux de la memoire* (1925), *Les Causes de suicide* (1930), *L'Evolution des besoins dans les classes ouvrières* (1933); died in deportation to Buchenwald.
Maurice Pradines (1874-1958): psychologist and philosopher; author of *Philosophie de la sensation* (1928-1934), *Esprit de la religion* (1941), *Traité de psychologie générale* (1943-1946), *L'Aventure de l'esprit dans les especes* (1955).
Henri Carteron (1891-1929): philosopher; translated Aristotle's *Physics*; author of *La Notion de Force dans le Système de Aristote* (1923). [Tr. note]

men! Naive exclamation returning to me in thought each time I evoke those so very rich years, and that nothing in my life has disappointed. Maurice Halbwachs had a martyr's death during the Occupation. In contact with these masters the great virtues of intelligence and intellectual probity were revealed to me, but also those of clarity and the elegance of the French university. Initiation into the great philosophers Plato and Aristotle, Descartes and the Cartesians, Kant. Not yet Hegel, in those twenties, at the Faculty of Arts of Strasbourg! But it was Durkheim and Bergson who seemed to me especially alive in the instruction and attention of the students. It was they whom one cited, and they whom one opposed. They had incontestably been the professors of our masters.

Ph.N.: Do you put the sociological thought of a Durkheim on the same level as the properly philosophical thought of a Bergson?

E.L.: Apparently, Durkheim was inaugurating an experimental sociology. But his work also appeared as a "rational sociology," as an elaboration of the fundamental categories of the social, as what one would call today an "eidetic of society," beginning with the leading idea that the social does not reduce to the sum of individual psychologies. Durkheim, a metaphysician! The idea that the social is the very order of the spiritual, a new plot in being above the animal and human psychism; the level of "collective representations" defined with vigor and which opens up the dimension of spirit in the individual life itself, where the individual alone comes to be recognized and even redeemed. In Durkheim there is, in a sense, a theory of "levels of being," of the irreducibility of these levels to one another, an idea which acquires its full meaning within the Husserlian and Heideggerian context.

Ph.N.: You have likewise mentioned Bergson. What, according to you, is his principal contribution to philosophy?

E.L.: The theory of duration. The destruction of the primacy of clock time; the idea that the time of physics is merely derived. Without this affirmation of the somehow "ontological" and not merely psychological priority of the duration irreducible to linear and homogenous time, Heidegger would not have been able to venture his conception of *Dasein's* finite temporalization, despite the radical difference which separates, of course, the Bergsonian conception of time from the Heideggerian conception. The credit goes back to Bergson for having liberated philosophy from the prestigious model of scientific time.

Ph.N.: But to what more personal question or anxiety has reading Bergson corresponded in you?

E.L.: Certainly to the fear of being in a world without novel possibilities, without a future of hope, a world where everything is regulated in advance; to the ancient fear before fate, be it that of a universal mechanism, absurd fate, since what is going to pass has in a sense already passed! Bergson, to the contrary, put forward the proper and irreducible reality of time. I do not know if the most modern science again confines us within a world with "nothing new." I think that at least science assures us of the renewal of its very horizons. But it is Bergson who taught us the spirituality of the new, "being" disengaged from the phenomenon in an "otherwise than being."

Ph.N.: When you completed your studies, what did you want to do in philosophy?

E.L.: To be sure, I wanted "to work in philosophy," but what could that mean outside of a purely pedagogical activity or the vanity of fabricating books? To do sociology as empirical science, which Durkheim called for and recommended to his students, and whose *a priori* he had elaborated? To repeat the completed, accomplished and perfect as a poem work of Bergson, or to present variations of it? It was with Husserl that I discovered the concrete meaning of the very possibility of "working in philosophy" without being straightaway enclosed in a system of dogmas, but at the same time without running the risk of proceeding by chaotic intuitions. The impression was at once of opening and method; the sentiment of the suitability and legitimacy of a questioning and philosophical inquiry which one would want to follow "without leaving the ranks." The formulation "philosophy as a rigorous science"[2] was without doubt the first attraction of his message. It was not through this somewhat formal promise that his work conquered me.

Ph.N.: How did you enter into contact with Husserl's work?

E.L.: By a pure accident. In Strasbourg, a young colleague, Miss Peiffer, with whom, later, we shared the translation of the Husserlian *Cartesian Meditations*,[3] and who prepared on Husserl what one then called the Dissertation of the Superior Studies Degree, had recommended to me a text which she was reading — I believe it was the *Logical Investigations*. I entered into that reading, at first very difficult,

2. Cf., Edmund Husserl, "Philosophy as Rigorous Science" (1911), in *Phenomenology and the Crisis of Philosophy*, transl. by Quintin Lauer (New York: Harper & Row, 1965), pp. 71-147. [Tr. note]
3. Edmond Husserl, *Meditations Cartésiennes*, transl. by Gabrielle Peiffer and Emmanuel Levinas, reviewed by Alexandre Koyré (Paris: Armand Coline, 1931; 2nd ed., Paris: J. Vrin, 1947). Meditations 4 and 5 (pp. 55-134) are translated by Levinas. [Tr. note]

with much diligence but also with much perseverance, and without guide. It was little by little that the
essential truth of Husserl, which I still believe today,
emerged into my mind, even if, in following his
method, I do not at all obey his school's percepts.

In the first place, there is the possibility *sich zu
besinnen*, of grasping oneself, or of getting back to oneself, of posing with distinctness the question: "Where
are we?", of taking ones bearings. Perhaps this is
phenomenology in the largest sense of the term,
beyond the vision of essences, the *Wesenschau* which
made such a fuss. A radical reflection, obstinate
about itself, a *cogito* which seeks and describes itself
without being duped by a spontaneity or ready-made
presence, in a major distrust toward what is thrust
naturally onto knowledge, a *cogito* which constitutes
the world and the object, but whose objectivity in
reality occludes and encumbers the look that fixes it.
From this objectivity one must always trace thoughts
and intentions back to the whole horizon at which
they aim, which objectivity obscures and makes one
forget. Phenomenology is the recall of these forgotten
thoughts, of these intentions; full consciousness, return to the misunderstood implied intentions of
thought in the world. This complete reflection is
necessary to the truth, even if its effective exercise
must in so doing make limits appear. It is the presence of the philosopher near to things, without
illusion or rhetoric, in their true status, precisely
clarifying this status, the meaning of their objectivity

and their being, not answering only to the question of knowing "What is?", but to the question "How *is* what is?", "What does it mean that it is?".

Recalling the obscured intentions of thought, the methodology of phenomenological work is also at the origin of some ideas which seem to me indispensable to all philosophical analysis. It is the new vigor given to the medieval idea of the intentionality of consciousness: all consciousness is consciousness of something, it is not describable without reference to the object it "claims." The intentional aim which is not a *knowledge*, but which in sentiments or aspirations, in its very dynamism, is qualified "affectively" or "actively." This is the first radical contestation in Western thought of the priority of the theoretical, which in Heidegger will be resumed with great brilliance in the description, notably, of the tool. Another idea correlative to intentionality, and equally characteristic of phenomenology is that the modes of consciousness having access to objects are *essentially* dependent on the essence of the object. God himself can know a material thing only by turning around it. Being commands the access to being. The access to being belongs to the description of being. I think that here also Heidegger is announced.

Ph.N.: For someone like yourself, however, who has centered all your work on metaphysics as ethics, there is apparently little to take directly from

Husserl, whose privileged domain of meditation is much rather the world and its constitution than man and his fate?

E.L.: You forget the importance in Husserl of axiological intentionality, of which I have just spoken. The character of value does not attach to beings consequent to the modification by *knowledge*, but comes from a specific attitude of consciousness, of a non-theoretical intentionality, straightoff irreducible to knowledge. There is here a Husserlian possibility which can be developed beyond what Husserl himself said on the ethical problem and on the relationship with the Other, which according to him remains representative (even though Merleau-Ponty tried to interpret it otherwise). The relationship with the Other can be sought as an irreducible intentionality, even if one must end by seeing that it ruptures intentionality.

Ph.N.: It is this that will be your path of thought. Did you know Husserl?

E.L.: For a year I audited his lectures at Fribourg. He had just retired, but he still taught. I was able to approach him and he received me amiably. At that time conversation with him, after some questions or replies by the student, was the monologue of the master concerned to call to mind the fundamental elements of his thought. But he sometimes also let himself go into particular original phenomenological analyses, referring to numerous unpublished manuscripts. The Husserl Archives of Louvain, organized and directed by my lamented and eminent friend, Father Van Breda, has rendered numerous of his pages readable and accessible. The courses I followed in 1928 bore on the notion of phenomenological psychology, and in the winter of 1928-29 on the constitution of intersubjectivity.

Two

Heidegger

Ph.N.: When you came to Fribourg to follow Husserl's teaching, you discovered there a philosopher you did not know beforehand, but who would have a capital importance in the elaboration of your thought: Martin Heidegger.

E.L.: I discovered in fact *Sein und Zeit*,[1] which people around me read. Very early I had a great admiration for this book. It is one of the finest books in the history of philosophy — I say this after years of reflection. One of the finest among four or five others . . .

Ph.N.: Which ones?

E.L.: For example, Plato's *Phædrus*, Kant's *Critique of Pure Reason*, Hegel's *Phenomenology of Mind*;

1. Martin Heidegger, *Being and Time*, transl. by J. Macquarrie and E. Robinson (New York: Harper and Row, 1962).

also Bergson's *Time and Free Will*. My admiration for Heidegger is above all an admiration for *Sein und Zeit*. I always try to relive the ambiance of those readings when 1933 was still unthinkable.

One speaks habitually of the word being as if it were a substantive, even though it is verb par excellence. In French, one says *the* being or *a* being. With Heidegger, "verbality" was awakened in the word being, what is event in it, the "happening" of being. It is as if things and all that is "set a style of being," "made a profession of being." Heidegger accustomed us to this verbal sonority. This reeducation of our ear is unforgetable, even if banal today. Philosophy would thus have been — even when it was not aware of it — an attempt to answer the question of the signification of being, as verb. While Husserl still proposed — or seemed to propose — a transcendental program for philosophy, Heidegger clearly defined philosophy in relation to other forms of knowledge as "fundamental ontology."

Ph.N.: What is ontology in this context?

E.L.: It is precisely the comprehension of the verb "to be." Ontology would be distinguished from all the disciplines which explore *that* which is, beings, that is, the "beings," their nature, their relations — while forgetting that in speaking of these beings they have already understood the meaning of the word being, without, however, having made it explicit. These disciplines do not worry about such an explication.

Ph.N.: *Sein und Zeit* appeared in 1927. Was this way of presenting the task of philosophy an absolute novelty at the time?

E.L.: That is in any case the impression that I have maintained of it. To be sure, in the history of philosophy it happens that after the fact one rediscovers the tendencies which retrospectively seem to announce the great innovations of today; but these consist at least in thematizing something which it was not beforehand. A thematization which requires genius and offers a new language.

The work that I did then on "the theory of intuition" in Husserl was thus influenced by *Sein und Zeit*, to the extent that I sought to present Husserl as having perceived the ontological problem of being, the question of the *status* rather than the *quiddity* of beings. Phenomenological analysis, I said, in searching for the constitution of the real for consciousness, does not undertake so much to search for transcendental conditions in the idealist sense of the term that it does not wonder about the signification of the being of "beings" in the diverse regions of knowledge.

In *Sein und Zeit*'s analyses of anxiety, care and being-toward-death, we witness a sovereign exercise of phenomenology. This exercise is extremely brilliant and convincing. It aims at describing man's being or existing — not his nature. What has been called existentialism has certainly been determined by *Sein und Zeit*. Heidegger did not like anyone to give his book this existentialist signification; human existence interested him only as the "place" of fundamental ontology; but the analysis of existence done in this book has marked and determined the analysis later called "existentialist."

Ph.N.: What struck you especially in Heidegger's phenomenological method?

E.L.: The intentionality animating existing itself and a whole series of "states of the soul" which, before Heideggerian phenomenology, passed for "blind," for simple contents; the pages on affectivity, on *Befindlichkeit* and, for example, on anxiety; anxiety appeared to banal study as an affective movement without cause or, more exactly, as "without object"; now it is precisely the fact of being without object which, in the Heideggerian analysis, shows itself to be truly significant. Anxiety would be the authentic and adequate access to nothingness, which could have seemed a derived notion to the philosophers, the result of a negation, and perhaps, as in Bergson, illusory. For Heidegger one does not "reach" nothingness through a series of theoretical steps, but, in anxiety, from a direct and irreducible access. Existence itself, as through the effect of an intentionality, is animated by a meaning, by the primordial onto-logical meaning of nothingness. It does not derive from what one can know *about* the destiny of man, or *about* his causes, or *about* his ends; existence in its very event of existence signifies, in anxiety, nothingness, as if the verb to exist had a direct complement.

Sein und Zeit has remained the very model of ontology. The Heideggerian notions of finitude, being-there, being-toward-death, etc., remain fundamental. Even if one frees oneself from the systematic rigors of this thought, one remains marked by the very style of *Sein und Zeit*'s analyses, by the "cardinal points" to which the "existential analytic" refers. I know that the homage I render to *Sein und Zeit* seems pale to the enthusiastic disciples of the great philosopher. But I think the later work of Heidegger, which does not produce in me a comparable impression, remains valuable through *Sein und Zeit*. Not, you well know, that it is insignificant; but it is much less convincing. I do not say this owing to Heidegger's political en-gagements, taken several years after *Sein und Zeit*, even though I have never forgotten those engage-ments, and though Heidegger has never been excul-pated in my eyes from his participation in Na-tional-Socialism.

Ph.N.: In what does the second part of the Heideggerian work disappoint you?

E.L.: Perhaps by the disappearance in it of phenomenology properly speaking; by the first place that the exigesis of Hölderlin's poetry and the etymologies began to occupy in his analysis. Of course, I know that in his thought the etymologies are not a contingency; for him language bears a wisdom which must be clarified. But this way of thinking seems to me much less verifiable than that of *Sein und Zeit* — a book in which, it is true, there are already etymologies, but adjacent and which only complete what is eminently strong in the analysis proper and in the phenomenology of existence.

Ph.N.: Language does not have this originary importance for you?

E.L.: In fact, for me, the *said* [*le dit*] does not count as much as the *saying* [*le dire*] itself. The latter is important to me less through its informational contents than by the fact that it is addressed to an interlocutor. But we will speak about this again. I think, despite these reservations, that a man who undertakes to philosophize in the twentieth century cannot not have gone through Heidegger's philosophy, even to escape it. This thought is a great event of our century. Philosophizing without having known Heidegger would involve a share of "naivité" in the Husserlian sense of the term. For Husserl there is very respectable and certain knowledge, scientific knowledge, which however is "naive" to the extent that, absorbed by the object, it ignores the problem of the status of its objectivity.

Ph.N.: You would say of Heidegger, all things being equal otherwise, what Sartre said of Marxism: that it is the unsurpassable horizon of our time?

E.L.: There are many things for which I can still not pardon Marx . . . In what concerns Heidegger, one cannot, in fact, ignore fundamental ontology and its problematic.

Ph.N.: Nevertheless there is a Heideggerian scholasticism today . . .

E.L.: . . . which takes the vicissitudes of the course for the ultimate reference of the thought.

I must underline still another essential contribution of Heidegger's thought: a new way of reading the history of philosophy. The philosophers of the past had already been saved from their archaism by Hegel. But they entered into "absolute thought" as moments, or as stages to go through; they were *aufgehoben*, that is, well and truly annihilated, at the same time as conserved. In Heidegger there is a new way, direct, of conversing with philosophers and asking for absolutely current teachings from the great classics. Of course, the philosopher of the past does not directly involve himself in the dialogue; there is an entire work of interpretation to accomplish in order to render him current. But in this hermeneutic one does not manipulate outworn things, one brings back the unthought to thought and saying.

Three

The "There Is"

Ph.N.: To begin with you were a historian of philosophy, or an analyst of other philosophers, since you published articles and works on Husserl and Heidegger. But the first book in which you express your own thought is a short work entitled *Existence and Existents*. In your preface you said you wrote it during the war, in the stalag. What is its subject?

E.L.: It deals with what I call the "there is" [*il y a*][1] I did not know Apollinaire had written a work entitled *There Is*. But for him the expression signifies the joy of what exists, the abundance, a little like the Heideggerian "*es gibt.*" For me, to the contrary,

1. In 1946 Levinas published an article entitled "Il y a" in *Deucalion* I (Cahiers de Philosophie) which was incorporated into the Introduction and Chapter 3, section 2 ("Existence without Existents") of *Existence and Existents*. [Tr. note]

"there is" is the phenomenon of impersonal being: "it." My reflection on this subject starts with childhood memories. One sleeps alone, the adults continue life; the child feels the silence of his bedroom as "rumbling."

Ph.N.: A rumbling silence?

E.L.: It is something resembling what one hears when one puts an empty shell close to the ear, as if the emptiness were full, as if the silence were a noise. It is something one can also feel when one thinks that even if there were nothing, the fact that "there is" is undeniable. Not that there is this or that; but the very scene of being is open: there is. In the absolute emptiness that one can imagine before creation — there is.

Ph.N.: A moment ago you evoked the "*es gibt*," the German "there is," and the analysis Heidegger made of it as generosity, since in this "*es gibt*" there is the verb *geben* which signifies to give. For you, on the other hand, there is no generosity in the "there is"?

E.L.: I insist in fact on the impersonality of the "there is"; "there is," as "it rains," or "its night." And there is neither joy nor abundance: it is a noise returning after every negation of this noise. Neither nothingness nor being. I sometimes use the expression: the excluded middle. One cannot say of this "there is" which persists that it is an event of being. One can neither say that it is nothingness, even though there is nothing. *Existence and Existents* tries to describe this horrible thing, and moreover describes it as horror and panic.

Ph.N.: The child who on his bed senses the night dragging on has an experience of horror . . .

E.L.: . . . Which nevertheless is not an anxiety. The book appeared with a wrapper where I had inscribed: "Where it is not a question of anxiety." Everyone began to speak alot about anxiety in Paris, in 1947 . . . Other experiences, all close to the "there is," are described in this book, notably that of insomnia. In insomnia one can and one cannot say that there is an "I" which cannot manage to fall asleep. The impossibility of escaping wakefulness is something "objective," independent of my initiative. This impersonality absorbs my consciousness; consciousness is depersonalized. I do not stay awake: "it" stays awake. Perhaps death is an absolute negation wherein "the music ends" (however, one knows nothing about it). But in the maddening "experience" of the "there is," one has the impression of a total impossibility of escaping it, of "stopping the music." It is a theme I have found in Maurice Blanchot, even though he does not speak of the "there is," but of the "neutral" or the "outside." He has a number of very suggestive formulas: he speaks of the "hustle-bustle" of being, of its "clamor," its "murmur." A night in a hotel room where, behind the partition, "it does not stop stirring"; "one does not know what they are doing next door." This is something very close to the "there is." It is not a matter of "states of the soul," but of an end of objectivizing consciousness, a psychological inversion. This is probably the real subject of his novels and stories.

Ph.N.: Do you mean to say that in Blanchot's works there is neither psychology nor sociology, but ontology? For in this "there is," whether it is horrible or not, what is at play is being?

E.L.: In Blanchot it is no longer being, and it is no longer "something," and it is always necessary to unsay what one says — it is an event which is neither being nor nothingness. In his last book,[2] Blanchot called this "disaster," which signifies neither death nor an accident, but as a piece of being which would be detached from its fixity of being, from its reference to a star, from all cosmological existence, a *dis-aster*. His gives an almost verbal sense to the substantive disaster. It seems that for him it is impossible to escape from this maddening, obsessive situation. In the short book of 1947 of which we are

2. *L'Ecriture du désastre* (Paris: Gallimard, 1981).

now speaking, as in that which followed it under the title of *Time and the Other* in 1948, the ideas to which I hold today are still sought, a good many of the intuitions arise which mark a distance covered rather than an ending. What is presented as exigency is an attempt to escape the "there is," to escape the non-sense. In *Existence and Existents*, I analyzed other modalities of being, taken in its verbal sense: fatigue, indolence, effort. In these phenomena I showed a dread before being, an impotent recoil, an evasion and, consequently, there too, the shadow of the "there is."

Ph.N.: What was the "solution" you proposed?

E.L.: My first idea was that perhaps a "being," a "something" one could point at with a finger, corresponds to a mastery over the "there is" which dreads in being. I spoke thus of the determinate being or existent as a dawn of clarity in the horror of the "there is," a moment where the sun rises, where things appear for themselves, where they are not borne by the "there is" but dominate it. Does one not say that the table is, that things are? Then one refastens being to the existent, and already the ego there dominates the existents it possesses. I spoke thus of the "hypostasis" of existents, that is, the passage going from *being* to a *something*, from the state of verb to the state of thing. Being which is posited, I thought, is "saved." In fact, this idea was only a first stage. For the ego that exists is encumbered by all these existents it dominates. For me the famous Heideggerian "Care" took the form of the cumbersomeness of existence.

From whence an entirely different movement: to escape the "there is" one must not be posed but deposed; to make an act of deposition, in the sense one speaks of deposed kings. This deposition of sovereignty by the *ego* is the social relationship with the Other, the dis-inter-ested relation. I write it in three words to underline the escape from being it signifies. I distrust the compromised word "love," but the responsibility for the Other, being-for-the-other, seemed to me, as early as that time, to stop the anonymous and senseless rumbling of being. It is in the form of such a relation that the deliverance from the "there is" appeared to me. Since that compelled my recognition and was clarified in my mind, I have hardly spoken again in my books of the "there is" for itself. But the shadow of the "there is," and of nonsense, still appeared to me necessary as the very test of dis-inter-estedness.

Four

The Solitude of Being

Ph.N.: After *Existence and Existents*, you wrote *Time and the Other*, a volume collecting four lectures given at Jean Wahl's College of Philosophy. Under what circumstances were you led to give these lectures?

E.L.: Jean Wahl — to whom I owe much — was on the lookout for everything that had a meaning, even outside the forms traditionally devoted to its manifestation. He was especially interested in the continuity between art and philosophy. He thought it was necessary, besides the Sorbonne, to give the opportunity for non-academic discourses to be heard. For this he thus founded this College in the Latin Quarter. It was a place where intellectual non-conformism — and even what took itself to be such — was tolerated and expected.

Ph.N.: Even though many minds in 1948 were occupied with the social aspect of problems, after the great unheaval which the war and Liberation had been, you were faithful to your metaphysical project?

E.L.: Certainly, but do not forget that it was the time when Jean-Paul Sartre and Maurice Merleau-Ponty dominated the philosophical horizon, when German phenomenology arrived in France, and when Heidegger began to be known. One did not only debate social problems; there was a sort of general opening and a curiosity about everything. I do not believe, however, that pure philosophy can be pure without going to the "social problem."

Time and the Other is a study of the relationship with the Other insofar as its element is time; as if time were transcendence, the opening par excellence onto the Other and onto the other. This thesis on transcendence, thought as dia-chrony, where the Same is non-in-different to the other without investing it in any way — not even by the most formal coincidence with it in a simple simultaneity — where the strangeness of the future is not described right-away in its reference to the present, where it would be to-come [à-venir] and where it was already anticipated in a pro-tention, this thesis (which preoccupies me much today) was, thirty years ago, only glimpsed. In *Time and the Other* it was treated starting from a series of more immediate evidences, which prepared some elements of the problem, such as I see it now.

Ph.N.: "The aim of these lectures," you write on the first page, "is to show that time is not the achievement of an isolated and lone subject, but that it is the subject's very relationship with the Other."[1] It is a strange way of beginning, for it supposes that solitude is in itself a problem.

E.L.: Solitude was an "existentialist" theme. At the time existence was described as the despair of solitude, or as the isolation within anxiety. The book represents an attempt to escape from this isolation of existing, as the preceding book signified an attempt to escape from the "there is." There also, there are two stages. First I examine an "exit" toward the world, in knowledge. My effort consists in showing that knowledge is in reality an immanence, and that there is no rupture of the isolation of being in knowledge; and on the other hand, that in the communication of knowledge one is found beside the Other, not confronted with him, not in the rectitude of the in-front-of him. But being in direct relation with the Other is not to thematize the Other and consider him in the same manner one considers a known object, nor to communicate a knowledge to him. In reality, the fact of being is what is most private; existence is the sole thing I cannot communicate; I can tell about it, but I cannot share my existence. Solitude thus

1. *Le Temps et l'Autre*, p. 17.

appears here as the isolation which marks the very event of being. The social is beyond ontology.

Ph.N.: You write: "It is banal to say we never exist in the singular. We are surrounded by beings and things with which we maintain relations. Through sight, touch, sympathy and common work we are *with* others. All these relations are transitive. I touch an object, I see the other; but I *am* not the other."[2]

E.L.: What is formulated here is the putting into question of this *with*, as possibility of escaping solitude. Does "existing with" represent a veritable sharing of existence? How is this sharing realized? Or again (for the word "sharing" would signify that existence is of the order of having): Is there a participation in being which makes us escape from solitude?

Ph.N.: One can only share what one has, one cannot share what one is?

E.L.: For that matter, the fundamental relation with being, in Heidegger, is not the relationship with the Other, but with death, where everything that is non-authentic in the relationship with the Other is denounced, since one dies alone.

2. *Le Temps et l'Autre*, p. 21.

Ph.N.: You follow: "I am all alone, it is thus the being in me, the fact that I exist, my existing, which constitutes the absolutely intransitive element, something without intentionality, without relation. One can exchange everything between beings, except existing. In this sense, to be is to be isolated by existing. I am monad inasmuch as I am. It is by existing that I am without doors or windows, and not through any content in me which would be incommunicable. If it is incommunicable it is that it is rooted in my being, which is what is most private in me. In this way, every enlargement of my consciousness, of my means of expression, remains without effect on my relation with existing, the interior relation par excellence."

E.L.: One must indeed understand nonetheless that solitude is not in itself the primary theme of these reflections. It is only one of the marks of being. It is not a matter of escaping from solitude, but rather of escaping *from being*.

Ph.N.: Thus, the first solution is the escaping from the self which constitutes the relation to the world in knowledge and in what you call "nourishments."

E.L.: By that I understand all terrestrial nourishments: the enjoyments through which the subject eludes his solitude. The very expression "to elude one's solitude" indicates the illusory and purely apparent character of this escape from the self. In what concerns knowledge: it is by essence a relation with what one equals and includes, with that whose alterity one suspends, with what becomes immanent, because it is to my measure and to my scale. I think of Descartes, who said that the *cogito* can give itself the sun and sky; the only thing it cannot give itself is the idea of the Infinite. Knowledge is always an adequation between thought and what it thinks. There is in knowledge, in the final account, an impossibility of escaping the self; hence sociality cannot have the same structure as knowledge.

Ph.N.: There is here something paradoxical. For the ordinary consciousness, to the contrary, knowledge is almost by definition what makes us escape ourselves. Even though you maintain that in knowledge, even of the stars, of what is farthest, we remain within the element of the "same"?

E.L.: Knowledge has always been interpreted as assimilation. Even the most surprising discoveries end by being absorbed, comprehended, with all that there is of "prehending" in "comprehending." The most audacious and remote knowledge does not put us in communion with the truly other; it does not take the place of sociality; it is still and always a solitude.

Ph.N.: You speak in this regard of knowledge as a light; what is illuminated is thus possessed.

E.L.: Or possessable. Up to the remotest stars.

Ph.N.: By distinction, the escape from solitude is going to be a dispossession or a detachment?

E.L.: Sociality will be a way of escaping being otherwise than through knowledge. In this book the demonstration is not dealt with in its entirety, but it is time which appeared to me then as an enlargement of existence. The book shows first some structures in the relationship with the Other which do not reduce to intentionality. It puts in doubt the Husserlian idea that intentionality represents the very spirituality of spirit. And the book tries to understand the role of time in this relationship: time is not a simple experience of duration, but a dynamism which leads us elsewhere than toward the things we possess. It is as if in time there were a movement beyond what is equal to us. Time as relationship to unattainable alterity and, thus, interruption of rhythm and its returns. The two principal analyses which support this thesis in *Time and the Other* concern, on the one hand, the erotic relationship, relationship — without confusion — with the alterity of the feminine, and, on the other hand, the relationship of paternity going from me to another who, in a certain sense, is still me and nevertheless is absolutely other: temporality brought near to the concreteness and logical paradox of fecundity. These are relationships with alterity which contrast strongly with those whereby the Same dominates or absorbs or includes the other, and whose model is knowledge.

Five

Love and Filiation

Ph.N.: The first analysis where the relation to the *other* breaks with the model of the subject taking cognizance of an object, would be that which concerns *eros*, despite the metaphors which suggest that love is knowledge. Would the alterity of the Other be significant as the future of time?

E.L.: In *eros* an alterity between things is exalted which does not reduce to the logical or numerical difference which formally distinguishes any individual from any other. But erotic alterity is not restricted either to that which, between comparable beings, is due to different attributes which distinguish them. The feminine is other for a masculine being not only because of a different nature but also inasmuch as alterity is in some way its nature. In the erotic relation is it not a matter of another attribute in the Other, but of an attribute of alterity in the Other. In *Time and the Other*, where the masculine and feminine are not thought in the neutral reciprocity which commands their inter-personal commerce, where the subject's ego is posited in its virility, and also where the ontological structure proper to femininity is studied (about which I will say a few words soon) — is this pure anachronism? — the feminine is described as the *of itself other*, as the origin of the very concept of alterity. What importance the ultimate pertinence of these views and the important correctives they demand have! They permit grasping in what sense, irreducible to that of numerical difference or a difference in nature, one can think the alterity which commands the erotic relation. Nothing in this relationship reduces the alterity that is exalted in it. Entirely opposed to knowledge which is suppression of alterity and which, in the "absolute knowledge" of Hegel, celebrates "the identity of the identical and the non-identical," alterity and duality do not disappear in the loving relationship. The idea of a love that would be a confusion between two beings is a false romantic idea. The pathos of the erotic relationship is the fact of being two, and that the other is absolutely other.

Ph.N.: This would be the not-knowing-the-Other that would make the relationship?

E.L.: The not-knowing is not to be understood here as a *privation* of knowledge. Unforeseeableness is a form of alterity only relative to knowledge. For it the other is essentially what is unforeseeable. But alterity, in *eros*, is not synonymous with unforeseeableness. It is not as a miscarried knowledge that love is love.

Ph.N.: Here are several lines from the chapter in *Time and the Other* devoted to the loving relationship: "The difference of sex is not the duality of two complementary terms. For two complementary terms presuppose a pre-existing whole. Now to say the sexual duality presupposes a whole is to posit in advance love as fusion. The pathos of love consists, to the contrary, in an insurmountable duality of beings; it is a relationship with what forever slips away. The relationship does not *ipso facto* neutralize alterity, but conserves it. [. . .] The other as other here is not an object which becomes ours or which becomes us, to the contrary, it withdraws into its mystery. [. . .] What matters to me in this notion of the feminine is not merely the unknowable, but a mode of being which consists in slipping away from the light. In existence the feminine is an event, different from that of spatial transcendence or expression which go toward the light; it is a flight before light. The way of existing of the feminine is hiding, or modesty. So this alterity of the feminine does not consist in the object's simple exteriority. Neither is it made of an opposition of wills."[1]

1. *Le Temps et l'Autre*, pp. 78-79.

". . . The transcendence of the feminine consists in withdrawing elsewhere, a movement opposed to the movement of consciousness. But this does not make it unconscious or subconscious, and I see no other possibility than to call it mystery. By positing the Other as freedom, by thinking it in terms of light, we are obliged to admit the failure of communication, that is, we have here only admitted the failure of the movement which tends to grasp or possess a freedom. It is only by showing in what way *eros* differs from possession and power that we can acknowledge a communication in *eros*. It is neither a struggle, nor a fusion, nor a knowledge. One must recognize its exceptional place among relations. It is the relationship with alterity, with mystery, that is, with the future, with what in the world where there is everything, is never there."[2]

E.L.: You see, this last proposition attests to the care of thinking time and the other together. Perhaps, on the other hand, all these allusions to the ontological differences between the masculine and the feminine would appear less archaic if, instead of dividing humanity into two species (or into two genders), they would signify that the participation in the masculine and in the feminine were the attribute of every human being. Could this be the meaning of

2. *Le Temps et l'Autre*, pp. 81.

the enigmatic verse of *Genesis* 1.27: "male and female created He them"?

Ph.N.: You follow with an analysis of voluptuosity: "What is caressed is not properly speaking touched. It is not the softness or tepidity of this hand given in contact that the caress seeks. It is this seeking of the caress which constitutes its essence, through the fact that the caress does not know what it seeks. This "not knowing," this fundamental disordering, is the essential. It is like a game with something slipping away, a game absolutely without project or plan, not with what can become ours or us, but with something other, always other, always inaccessible, and always to come. And the caress is the anticipation of this pure future without content."[3]

There is a second type of relationship with the Other which is not a relation of knowledge, and authentically realizes the escape out of being, and which itself also implies the dimension of time: filiality.

E.L.: Filiality is still more mysterious: it is a relationship with the Other where the Other is radically other, and where nevertheless it is in some way me; the father's ego has to do with an alterity which is his, without being a possession or a property.

3.   *Le Temps et l'Autre*, pp. 82.

Ph.N.: You say that the son represents possibilities which are impossible for the father and which nonetheless are *his* possibilities?

E.L.: At Jean Wahl's I once delivered a lecture on filiality which I entitled "Beyond the Possible," as if my being, in fecundity — and starting from the children's possibilities — exceeded the possibilities inscribed in the nature of a being. I would like to underline the upheaval — that this signifies — of the ontological condition and also of the logic of substance, on the one hand, and of transcendental subjectivity, on the other.

Ph.N.: You see in this a properly ontological feature and not merely a psychological accident or perhaps a ruse of biology?

E.L.: I believe that psychological "accidents" are the ways in which ontological relations show themselves. Psychology not a peripety.

The fact of seeing the possibilities of the other as your own possibilities, of being able to escape the closure of your identity and what is bestowed on you, toward something which is not bestowed on you and which nevertheless is yours — this is paternity. This future beyond my own being, this dimension constitutive of time, takes on a concrete content in paternity. It is not necessary that those who have no children see in this fact any depreciation whatever;

biological filiality is only the first shape filiality takes; but one can very well conceive filiality as a relationship between human beings without the tie of biological kinship. One can have a paternal attitude with regard to the Other. To consider the Other as a son is precisely to establish with him those relations I call "beyond the possible."

Ph.N.: Can you give examples of these spiritual filiations? Is there something like this in the relation of master to disciple?

E.L.: Filiation and fraternity — parental relations without biological bases — are current metaphors of our everyday life. The relationship of master to disciple does not reduce to filiation and fraternity, but it certainly includes them.

Ph.N.: You write: "Paternity is a relationship with a stranger who, entirely while being Other, is me. It is the relationship of the ego with a selfsame ego who is nonetheless a stranger to the ego. The son in fact is not simply my work, like a poem or manufactured object, neither is he my property. Neither the categories of power nor those of having can indicate the relationship with a child. Neither the notion of cause nor the notion of ownership permit grasping the fact of fecundity. I do not have my child, I *am* in some way my child. Only the words "I am" here have a signification different from the Eleatic or Platonic signification. There is a multiplicity and a transcendence in the verb to exist, a transcendence which is lacking to even the boldest existentialist analyses. Moreover, the son is not any event whatsoever that happens to me, as for example my sadness, my trial or my suffering. It is an ego, a person. Lastly, the alterity of the son is not that of an *alter ego*; paternity is not some sympathy through which I can put myself in the son's place; it is through my being that I am my son and not through sympathy. [. . .] It is not according to the category of cause, but according to the category of the father that freedom occurs and time is accomplished. [. . .] Paternity is not simply a renewal of the father in the son and his confusion with him. It is also the exteriority of the father in relation to the son. It is a pluralist existing."[4]

4. *Le Temps et l'Autre*, pp. 82-87.

Six

Secrecy and Freedom

Ph.N.: We will speak today about *Totality and Infinity*, a book dated 1961 which, with *Otherwise than Being or Beyond Essence*, is one of your principal works of philosophy. The title contains in itself a problem or a question. In what are "totality" and "infinity" opposed to one another?

E.L.: In the critique of totality borne by the very association of these two words, there is a reference to the history of philosophy. This history can be interpreted as an attempt at universal synthesis, a reduction of all experience, of all that is reasonable, to a totality wherein consciousness embraces the world, leaves nothing other outside of itself, and thus becomes absolute thought. The consciousness of self is at the same time the consciousness of the whole. There have been few protestations in the history of philosophy against this totalization. In what concerns me, it is in Franz Rosenzweig's philosophy, which is essentially a discussion of Hegel, that for the first time I encountered a radical critique of totality. This critique starts from the experience of death; to the extent that the individual included within the totality has not vanquished the anxiety about death, nor renounced his particular destiny, he does not find himself at ease within the totality or, if you will, the totality has not "totalized" itself. In Rosenzweig there is thus an explosion of the totality and the opening of quite a different route in the search for what is reasonable.

Ph.N.: A route that Western philosophy has not explored, and to which it has heavily preferred that of systems?

E.L.: It is in fact the whole trend of Western philosophy culminating in the philosophy of Hegel, which, for very good reason, can appear as the culmination of philosophy itself. One can see this nostalgia for totality everywhere in Western philosophy, where the spiritual and the reasonable always reside in knowledge. It is as if the totality had been lost, and that this loss were the sin of the mind. It is then the panoramic vision of the real which is the truth and which gives all its satisfaction to the mind.

Ph.N.: This globalizing vision, which thus characterizes the great philosophical systems, appears to you to be an affront to another experience of meaning?

E.L.: The irreducible and ultimate experience of relationship appears to me in fact to be elsewhere: not in synthesis, but in the face to face of humans, in sociality, in its moral signification. But it must be understood that morality comes not as a secondary layer, above an abstract reflection on the totality and its dangers; morality has an independent and preliminary range. First philosophy is an ethics.

Ph.N.: Opposing the idea that one can ultimately totalize all meaning within a single knowledge, there are things you call "non-synthesizables." These will thus be the ethical situations?

E.L.: The relationship between men is certainly the non-synthesizable par excellence. One can also wonder if the idea of God, especially such as Descartes thinks it, can be made part of a totality of being, or if it is not, much rather, transcendent to being. The term "transcendence" signifies precisely the fact that one cannot think God and being together. So too in the interpersonal relationship it is not a matter of thinking the ego and the other together, but to be facing. The true union or true togetherness is not a togetherness of synthesis, but a togetherness of face to face.

Ph.N.: There is another example of the non-synthesizable that you cite in the book. A human life, with birth and death, can be written about by someone else, by someone who is thus not dead, who you call the survivor or historian. Now everyone perceives that there is an irreducible difference between the course of one's life and what in it will then be registered in the chronological succession of the events of history and the world. My life and history thus do not form a totality?

E.L.: Indeed, the two points of view are absolutely non-synthesizable. That sphere of the common which every synthesis presupposes is absent between men. The common element which permits us to speak of an objectified society, and through which man resembles things and individualizes himself like a thing, is not primary. The true human subjectivity is indescernable, according to Leibniz's expression, and consequently it is not as the individuals of a genus that men are together. One has always known this in speaking of the secrecy of subjectivity; but this secrecy has been ridiculed by Hegel: speaking thus was good for romantic thought . . .

Ph.N.: In the thoughts of the totality there is totalitarianism since there secrecy is inadmissible?

E.L.: My critique of the totality has come in

fact after a political experience that we have not yet forgotten.

Ph.N.: Let's speak of political philosophy. In *Totality and Infinity*, you try to ground "sociality" in something other than a global and synthetic concept of "the" society. You write this sentence: "The real must not only be determined in its historical objectivity, but also from interior intentions, from the secrecy that interrupts the continuity of historical time. Only starting from this secrecy is the pluralism of society possible."[1] A society respectful of freedoms would thus not simply have "liberalism" for its foundation, an objective theory of society which posits that society functions best when one lets things go liberally. Such a liberalism would make freedom depend on an objective principle and not on the essential secrecy of lives. Freedom would then be but entirely relative: it would suffice that one objectively prove the greater efficiency, from a political or economic point of view, of a given type of organization, for freedom to remain speechless. To ground an authentically free society nothing less is necessary than the metaphysical idea of "secrecy"?

E.L.: *Totality and Infinity* is my first book which goes in that direction. It aims to pose the problem of the intersubjective relationship's content. For what

1. *Totalité et infini*, p. 29/ *Totality and Infinity*, pp. 57-58.

we have said up to now is only negative. What positively does this "sociality" different from total and additive sociality consist in? It is this that preoccupied me in what followed. The sentence you read remains still rather formal in relation to what today appears to me as the essential.

For it is not necessary, from what I have just said, to deduce any underestimation of reason and reason's aspiration to universality. I only try to deduce the necessity for a social rationale of the very exigencies of the intersubjective such as I describe it. It is extremely important to know if society in the current sense of the term is the result of a limitation of the principle that men are predators of one another, or if to the contrary it results from the limitation of the principle that men are *for* one another. Does the social, with its institutions, universal forms and laws, result from limiting the consequences of the war between men, or from limiting the infinity which opens in the ethical relationship of man to man?

Ph.N.: In the first case, one has a conception of the political which makes it an internal regulation of society, as in a society of bees or ants; it is a naturalist and "totalitarian" conception. In the second case, there is a higher regulation, of another nature, ethical, standing above politics?

E.L.: Politics must be able in fact always to be checked and criticized starting from the ethical. This second form of sociality would render justice to that secrecy which for each is his life, a secrecy which does not hold to a closure which would isolate some rigorously private domain of a closed interiority, but a secrecy which holds to the responsibility for the Other. This would be a responsibility which is inaccessible in its ethical advent, from which one does not escape, and which, thus, is the principle of an absolute individuation.

Seven

The Face

Ph.N.: In *Totality and Infinity* you speak at great length of the face. It is one of your frequent themes. What does this phenomenology of the face, that is, this analysis of what happens when I look at the Other face to face, consist in and what is its purpose?

E.L.: I do not know if one can speak of a "phenomenology" of the face, since phenomenology describes what appears. So, too, I wonder if one can speak of a look turned toward the face, for the look is knowledge, perception. I think rather that access to the face is straightaway ethical. You turn yourself toward the Other as toward an object when you see a nose, eyes, a forehead, a chin, and you can describe them. The best way of encountering the Other is not even to notice the color of his eyes! When one observes the color of the eyes one is not in social relationship with the Other. The relation with the face can surely be dominated by perception, but what is specifically the face is what cannot be reduced to that.

There is first the very uprightness of the face, its upright exposure, without defense. The skin of the face is that which stays most naked, most destitute. It is the most naked, though with a decent nudity. It is the most destitute also: there is an essential poverty in the face; the proof of this is that one tries to mask this poverty by putting on poses, by taking on a countenance. The face is exposed, menaced, as if inviting us to an act of violence. At the same time, the face is what forbids us to kill.

Ph.N.: War stories tell us in fact that it is difficult to kill someone who looks straight at you.

E.L.: The face is signification, and signification without context. I mean that the Other, in the rectitude of his face, is not a character within a context. Ordinarily one is a "character": a professor at the Sorbonne, a Supreme Court justice, son of so-and-so, everything that is in one's passport, the manner of dressing, of presenting oneself. And all signification in the usual sense of the term is relative to such a context: the meaning of something is in its relation to another thing. Here, to the contrary, the face is meaning all by itself. You are you. In this sense one can say that the face is not "seen". It is what cannot become a content, which your thought would embrace; it is uncontainable, it leads you beyond. It is in this that the signification of the face makes it escape from being, as a correlate of a knowing. Vision, to the contrary, is a search for adequation; it is what par excellence absorbs being. But the relation to the face is straightaway ethical. The face is what one cannot kill, or at least it is that whose *meaning* consists in saying: "thou shalt not kill." Murder, it is true, is a banal fact: one can kill the Other; the ethical exigency is not an ontological necessity. The prohibition against killing does not render murder impossible, even if the authority of the prohibition is maintained in the bad conscience about the accomplished evil — malignancy of evil. It also appears in the Scriptures, to which the humanity of man is exposed inasmuch as it is engaged in the world. But to speak truly, the appearance in being of these "ethical peculiarities" — the humanity of man — is a rupture of being. It is significant, even if being resumes and recovers itself.

Ph.N.: The Other is face; but the Other, equally, speaks to me and I speak to him. Is not human discourse another way of breaking what you call "totality"?

E.L.: Certainly. Face and discourse are tied. The face speaks. It speaks, it is in this that it renders possible and begins all discourse. I have just refused the notion of vision to describe the authentic relationship with the Other; it is discourse and, more exactly, response or responsibility which is this authentic relationship.

Ph.N.: But since the ethical relationship is beyond knowledge, and, on the other hand, it is authentically assumed through discourse, it is thus that discourse itself is not something of the order of knowledge?

E.L.: In discourse I have always distinguished, in fact, between the *saying* and the *said*. That the *saying* must bear a *said* is a necessity of the same order as that which imposes a society with laws, institutions and social relations. But the *saying* is the fact that before the face I do not simply remain there contemplating it, I respond to it. The saying is a way of greeting the Other, but to greet the Other is already to answer for him. It is difficult to be silent in someone's presence; this difficulty has its ultimate foundation in this signification proper to the saying, whatever is the said. It is necessary to speak of something, of the rain and fine weather, no matter what, but to speak, to respond to him and already to answer for him.

Ph.N.: In the face of the Other you say there is an "elevation," a "height." The Other is higher than I am. What do you mean by that?

THE FACE

E.L.: The first word of the face is the "Thou shalt not kill." It is an order. There is a commandment in the appearance of the face, as if a master spoke to me. However, at the same time, the face of the Other is destitute; it is the poor for whom I can do all and to whom I owe all. And me, whoever I may be, but as a "first person," I am he who finds the resources to respond to the call.

Ph.N.: One is tempted to say to you: yes, in certain cases. But in other cases, to the contrary, the encounter with the Other occurs in the mode of violence, hate and disdain.

E.L.: To be sure. But I think that whatever the motivation which explains this inversion, the analysis of the face such as I have just made, with the mastery of the Other and his poverty, with my submission and my wealth, is primary. It is the presupposed in all human relationships. If it were not that, we would not even say, before an open door, "After you, sir!" It is an original "After you, sir!" that I have tried to describe.

You have spoken of the passion of hate. I feared a much graver objection: How is it that one can punish and repress? How is it that there is justice? I answer that it is the fact of the multiplicity of men and the presence of someone else next to the Other, which condition the laws and establish justice. If I am alone with the Other, I owe him everything; but there is someone else. Do I know what my neighbor is in relation to someone else? Do I know if someone else has an understanding with him or his victim? Who is my neighbor? It is consequently necessary to weigh, to think, to judge, in comparing the incomparable. The interpersonal relation I establish with the Other, I must also establish with other men; there is thus a necessity to moderate this privilege of the Other; from whence comes justice. Justice, exercised through institutions, which are inevitable, must always be held in check by the initial interpersonal relation.

Ph.N.: The crucial experience is thus here in your metaphysics: that which permits escaping Heidegger's ontology as an ontology of the Neutral, an ontology without morals. Is it starting from this ethical experience that you construct an "ethics"? For it follows, ethics is made up of rules; it is necessary to establish these rules?

E.L.: My task does not consist in constructing ethics; I only try to find its meaning. In fact I do not believe that all philosophy should be programmatic. It is Husserl above all who brought up the idea of a program of philosophy. One can without doubt construct an ethics in function of what I have just said, but this is not my own theme.

Ph.N.: Can you specify in what this discovery of ethics in the face breaks with the philosophies of totality?

E.L.: Absolute knowledge, such as it has been sought, promised or recommended by philosophy, is a thought of the Equal. Being is embraced in the truth. Even if the truth is considered as never definitive, there is a promise of a more complete and adequate truth. Without doubt, the finite being that we are cannot in the final account complete the task of knowledge; but in the limit where this task is accomplished, it consists in making the other become the Same. On the other hand, the idea of the Infinite implies a thought of the Unequal. I start from the Cartesian idea of the Infinite, where the *ideatum* of this idea, that is, what this idea aims at, is infinitely greater than the very act through which one thinks it. There is a disproportion between the act and that to which the act gives access. For Descartes, this is one of the proofs of God's existence: thought cannot produce something which exceeds thought; this something had to be put into us. One must thus admit to an infinite God who has put the idea of the Infinite into us. But it is not the proof Descartes sought that interests me here. I am thinking here of the astonishment at this disproportion between what he calls the "objective reality" and the "formal reality" of the idea of God, of the very paradox — so anti-Greek — of an idea "put" into me, even though Socrates taught us that it is impossible *to put* an idea into a thought without it already having been found there.

Now, in the face such as I describe its approach, is produced the same exceeding of the act by that to which it leads. In the access to the face there is certainly also an access to the idea of God. In Descartes the idea of the Infinite remains a theoretical idea, a contemplation, a knowledge. For my part, I think that the relation to the Infinite is not a knowledge, but a Desire. I have tried to describe the difference between Desire and need by the fact that Desire cannot be satisfied; that Desire in some way nourishes itself on its own hungers and is augmented by its satisfaction; that Desire is like a thought which thinks more than it thinks, or more than what it thinks. It is a paradoxical structure, without doubt, but one which is no more so than this presence of the Infinite in a finite act.

Eight

Responsibility for the Other

Ph.N.: In your last great book published, *Otherwise than Being or Beyond Essence*, you speak of moral responsibility. Husserl had already spoken of responsibility, but of a responsibility for the truth; Heidegger had spoken of authenticity; as for yourself, what do you understand by responsibility?

E.L.: In this book I speak of responsibility as the essential, primary and fundamental structure of subjectivity. For I describe subjectivity in ethical terms. Ethics, here, does not supplement a preceding existential base; the very node of the subjective is knotted in ethics understood as responsibility.

I understand responsibility as responsibility for the Other, thus as responsibility for what is not my deed, or for what does not even matter to me; or which precisely does matter to me, is met by me as face.

Ph.N.: How, having discovered the Other in his face, does one discover him as he to whom one is responsible?

E.L.: In describing the face positively, and not merely negatively. You recall what we said: meeting the face is not of the order of pure and simple perception, of the intentionality which goes toward adequation. Positively, we will say that since the Other looks at me, I am responsible for him, without even having *taken* on responsibilities in his regard; his responsibility *is incumbent on me*. It is responsibility that goes beyond what I do. Usually, one is responsible for what one does oneself. I say, in *Otherwise than Being*, that responsibility is initially a *for the Other*. This means that I am responsible for his very responsibility.

Ph.N.: What in this responsibility for the Other defines the structure of subjectivity?

E.L.: Responsibility in fact is not a simple attribute of subjectivity, as if the latter already existed in itself, before the ethical relationship. Subjectivity is not for itself; it is, once again, initially for another. In the book, the proximity of the Other is presented as the fact that the Other is not simply close to me in space, or close like a parent, but he approaches me essentially insofar as I feel myself — insofar as I am — responsible for him. It is a structure that in nowise resembles the intentional relation

which in knowledge attaches us to the object — to no
matter what object, be it a human object. Proximity
does not revert to this intentionality; in particular it
does not revert to the fact that the Other is known to me.

Ph.N.: I can know someone to perfection, but
this knowledge will never by itself be a proximity?

E.L.: No. The tie with the Other is knotted
only as responsibility, this moreover, whether ac-
cepted or refused, whether knowing or not knowing
how to assume it, whether able or unable to do
something concrete for the Other. To say: here I am
[*me voici*].[1] To do something for the Other. To give.
To be human spirit, that's it. The incarnation of
human subjectivity guarantees its spirituality (I do
not see what angels could give one another or how
they could help one another). Dia-chrony before all
dialogue: I analyze the inter-human relationship as
if, in proximity with the Other — beyond the image I
myself make of the other man — his face, the ex
pressive in the Other (and the whole human body is
in this sense more or less face), were what *ordains* me
to serve him. I employ this extreme formulation. The
face orders and ordains me. Its signification is an

1. Cf., *Genesis* 22, lines 1, 7 and 11, and *Isaiah* 6, line 8, for *Hineni*.
   Also, cf., Emmanuel Levinas, "God and Philosophy," in *Philosophy Today*, Vol. XXII, no. 2, Summer 1978, pp. 127-145. [Tr.
   note]

order signified. To be precise, if the face signifies an order in my regard, this is not in the manner in which an ordinary sign signifies its signified; this order is the very signifyingness of the face.

Ph.N.: You say at once "it orders me" and "it ordains me." Is this not a contradiction?

E.L.: It orders me as one orders someone one commands, as when one says: "Someone's asking for you."

Ph.N.: But is not the Other also responsible in my regard?

E.L.: Perhaps, but that is *his* affair. One of the fundamental themes of *Totality and Infinity* about which we have not yet spoken is that the intersubjective relation is a non-symmetrical relation. In this sense, I am responsible for the Other without waiting for reciprocity, were I to die for it. Reciprocity is *his* affair. It is precisely insofar as the relationship between the Other and me is not reciprocal that I am subjection to the Other; and I am "subject" essentially in this sense. It is I who support all. You know that sentence in Dostoyevsky: "*We are all guilty of all and for all men before all, and I more than the others.*"[1] This

2. Cf., Fyodor Dostoyevsky, *The Brothers Karamazov*, transl. by Constance Garnett (New York: New American Library, 1957), p. 264.

is not owing to such or such a guilt which is really mine, or to offenses that I would have committed; but because I am responsible for a total responsibility, which answers for all the others and for all in the others, even for their responsibility. The I always has one responsibility *more* than all the others.

Ph.N.: That means that if the others do not do what they ought to do, it is owing to me?

E.L.: I have previously said elsewhere — I do not like mentioning it for it should be completed by other considerations — that I am responsible for the persecutions that I undergo. But only me! My "close relations" or "my people" are already the others and, for them, I demand justice.

Ph.N.: You go that far!

E.L.: Since I am responsible even for the Other's responsibility. These are extreme formulas which must not be detached from their context. In the concrete, many other considerations intervene and require justice even for me. Practically, the laws set certain consequences out of the way. But justice only has meaning if it retains the spirit of dis-inter-estedness which animates the idea of responsibility for the other man. In principle the I does not pull itself out of its "first person"; it supports the world.

Constituting itself in the very movement wherein being responsible for the other devolves on it, subjectivity goes to the point of substitution for the Other. It assumes the condition — or the uncondition — of hostage. Subjectivity as such is initially hostage; it answers to the point of expiating for others.

One can appear scandalized by this utopian and, for an I, inhuman conception. But the humanity of the human — the true life — is absent. The humanity in historical and objective being, the very breakthrough of the subjective, of the human psychism in its original vigilance or sobering up, is being which undoes its condition of being: dis-inter-*estedness*. This is what is meant by the title of the book: *Otherwise than Being*. The ontological condition undoes itself, or is undone, in the human condition or uncondition. To be human means to live as if one were not a being among beings. As if, through human spirituality, the categories of being inverted into an "otherwise than being." Not only into a "being otherwise"; being otherwise is still being. The "otherwise than being," in truth, has no verb which would designate the event of its un-rest, its dis-inter-*estedness*, its putting-into-question of this being — or this *estedness* — of the being.

It is I who support the Other and am responsible for him. One thus sees that in the human subject, at the same time as a total subjection, my primogeniture manifests itself. My responsibility is untransferable, no one could replace me. In fact, it is a matter of saying the very identity of the human I starting from responsibility, that is, starting from this position or deposition of the sovereign I in self consciousness, a deposition which is precisely its responsibility for the Other. Responsibility is what is incumbent on me exclusively, and what, *humanly*, I cannot refuse. This charge is a supreme dignity of the unique. I am I in the sole measure that I am responsible, a non-interchangeable I. I can substitute myself for everyone, but no one can substitute himself for me. Such is my inalienable identity of subject. It is in this precise sense that Dostoyevsky said: "*We are all responsible for all for all men before all, and I more than all the others.*"

Nine

The Glory of Testimony

Ph.N.: The ethical relationship makes us escape the "solitude" of being. But if we are then no longer in being, are we only in a society?

E.L.: You are thinking: what becomes of the Infinity that the title *Totality and Infinity* announced? I am not afraid of the word God, which appears quite often in my essays. To my mind the Infinite comes in the signifyingness of the face. The face *signifies* the Infinite. It never appears as a theme, but in this ethical signifyingness itself; that is, in the fact that the more I am just the more I am responsible, one is never quits with regard to the Other.

Ph.N.: There is an infinity in the ethical exigency in that it is insatiable?

E.L.: Yes. It is the exigency of holiness. At no time can one say: I have done all my duty. Except the hypocrite . . . It is in this sense that there is an opening beyond what is delimited; and such is the manifestation of the Infinite. It is not a "manifestation" in the sense of "disclosure," which would be adequation to a given. On the contrary, the characteristic of the relation to the Infinite is that it is not disclosure. When in the presence of the Other, I say "Here I am!", this "Here I am!" is the place through which the Infinite enters into language, but without giving itself to be seen. Since it is not thematized, in any case originally, it does not appear. The "invisible God" is not to be understood as God invisible to the senses, but as God non-thematizable in thought, and nonetheless as non-indifferent to the thought which is not thematization, and probably not even an intentionality.

I am going to tell you a peculiar feature of Jewish mysticism. In certain very old prayers, fixed by ancient authorities, the faithful one begins by saying to God "Thou" and finishes the proposition thus begun by saying "He," as if, in the course of this approach of the "Thou" its transcendence into "He" supervened. It is what in my descriptions I have called the "illeity" of the Infinite. Thus, in the "Here I am!" of the approach of the Other, the Infinite does not show itself. How then does it take on meaning? I will say that the subject who says "Here I am!" *testifies* to the Infinite. It is through this testimony, whose truth is not the truth of representation or perception, that the revelation of the Infinite occurs.

It is through this testimony that the very glory of the Infinite glorifies *itself*. The term "glory" does not belong to the language of contemplation.

Ph.N.: But wait: who testifies to what and to whom in testimony? What has the witness or the prophet of whom you speak seen happen, about which he has to render testimony?

E.L.: You continue here to think of testimony as based on knowledge and thematization. The concept of testimony I am trying to describe surely implies a mode of revelation, but this revelation *gives* us nothing. Philosophical speech as such always comes back to a thematization . . .

Ph.N.: . . . however one could ask you why you yourself thematize all this, and at this very moment. Is this not also in a sense to testify?

E.L.: Naturally I have myself made this objection. I have spoken somewhere of the philosophical *saying* as a saying which is in the necessity of always unsaying itself. I have even made this unsaying a proper mode of philosophizing. I do not deny that philosophy is a knowledge, insofar as it names even what is not nameable, and thematizes what is not thematizable. But in thus giving to what breaks with the categories of discourse the form of the *said*, perhaps it impresses onto the said the traces of this rupture.

Ethical testimony is a revelation which is not a knowledge. Must one still say that in this mode one only "testifies" to the Infinite, to God, about which no presence or actuality is *capable* of testifying. The philosophers said there is no present infinite. What may pass for a "fault" of the infinite is to the contrary a positive characteristic of it — its very infinity.

In *Otherwise than Being or Beyond Essence* I wrote this: "The subject, or the other in the Same, insofar as the Same is for the other, testifies to the Infinite, of which no theme, no present, is capable. Here the difference is absorbed in the measure that proximity is made closer and through this very absorption stands out gloriously and always accuses me more. Here the Same, in its bearing as Same, is more and more extended with regard to the other, extended up to substitution as hostage, in an expiation which coincides in the final account with the extraordinary and diachronic reversal of the Same into the other in inspiration and psychism."[1] I mean that this way in which the other or the Infinite manifests itself in subjectivity is the very phenomenon of "inspiration," and consequently defines the psychic element, the very pneumatic of the psychism.

Ph.N.: That is to say, the Spirit. Thus, if God

1. *Autrement qu'être*, pp. 186-187/*Otherwise than Being*, p. 146.

is not seen, he has testimony rendered to Himself; if he is not thematized, he is attested.

E.L.: The witness testifies to what was said by himself. For he has said "Here I am!" before the Other; and from the fact that before the Other he recognizes the responsibility which is incumbent on himself, he has manifested what the face of the Other signified for him. The glory of the Infinite reveals itself through what it is capable of doing in the witness.

Ph.N.: For to say "Here I am!" even though life seems to go in an entirely contrary direction, since life only wants itself and commands only persistence in being, is by contrast to manifest something superior to life and death, thus glorious . . .

E.L.: The "otherwise than being" is the glory of God. "The idea of the Infinite which in Descartes is lodged in a thought that cannot contain it, expresses the disproportion between glory and the present, a disproportion which is inspiration itself. Under the weight that exceeds my capacity, a passivity more passive than all passivity correlative of acts, my passivity breaks out in saying: "Here I am!" The exteriority of the Infinite somehow becomes "interiority" in the sincerity of the testimony."[2]

2. *Autrement qu'être*, p. 187/*Otherwise than Being*, pp. 146-147.

Ph.N.: For want of being known, the infinite is absorbed?

E.L.: No. It commands.

Ph.N.: At least in this sense it is not exterior: it has decisively approached.

E.L.: Indeed; it commands and in this sense it is interior. "The glory which does not affect me as a representation or as an interlocutor before which and before whom I put myself, glorifies itself in my saying, commanding me through my mouth. Interiority is consequently not a secret place somewhere in me. It is that reverting in which the eminently exterior, precisely in virtue of this eminent exteriority, this impossibility of being contained and consequently entering into a theme, infinite exception to essence, concerns me and circumscribes me and orders me by my own voice. The commandment is stated through the mouth of him it commands, the infinitely exterior becomes an interior voice, but a voice testifying to the fission of the interior secrecy, signalling to the Other. Sign of this very donation of the sign. Crooked road. Claudel chose as an epigraph for his *Satin Slipper* a Portuguese proverb that can be understood in the sense I have just put forth: 'God writes straight with crooked lines.' "[3]

3. *Autrement qu'être*, p. 187/*Otherwise than Being*, p. 147.

Ten

*The Hardness of Philosophy
and the
Consolations of Religion*

Ph.N.: Is there not an indirect definition of prophetism in this insistance upon testimony, irreducible to a thematizing knowledge?

E.L.: Prophetism is in fact the fundamental mode of revelation — on condition one understands prophetism in a very much larger sense than that admitted by the gift, the talent or the special vocation of those whom one calls the prophets. I think prophetism as a moment of the human condition itself. For every man, assuming responsibility for the Other is a way of testifying to the glory of the Infinite, and of being inspired. There is prophetism and inspiration in the man who answers for the Other, paradoxically, even before knowing what is concretely required of himself. This responsibility prior to the Law is God's revelation. There is a text of the prophet Amos that says: "God has spoken, who would not prophecy?",[1]

1. *Amos*, 3.8.

where prophecy seems posited as the fundamental fact of man's humanity. This being so, next to the unlimited ethical exigency, prophecy interprets itself in concrete forms, where it has become book and text. In these concrete forms, become religions, men find consolations. But this by no means puts the rigorous structure I have tried to define back into doubt; in which it is always I who am responsible and I who support the universe, whatever happens next.

Apropos of these few reflections I have just set forth, I was once asked if the messianic idea still had meaning for me, and if it were necessary to retain the idea of an ultimate stage of history where humanity would no longer be violent, where humanity would have broken definitely through the crust of being, and where everything would be clear. I answered that to be worthy of the messianic era one must admit that ethics has a meaning, even without the promises of the Messiah.

Ph.N.: The positive religions, or at the least the three great religions of the Book recognized in the West, are each defined by the relation to a definitely established text, containing the Revelation; now when you speak of the "revelation" brought about by "testimony" you seem to find another origin for religious truth, and in the very present.

E.L.: What I say here of course only commits me! It is on these grounds that I answer this question. I am convinced that the Bible is the outcome of prophecies and that in it ethical testimony — I do not say "experience" — is deposited in the form of writings. But this perfectly agrees with the humanity of man as responsibility for the Other which has been set forth in our interviews. That modern historical criticism has shown that the Bible had multiple authors spread over very different periods, contrary to what was believed several centuries ago, changes nothing of this conviction, to the contrary. For I have always thought that the great miracle of the Bible lies not at all in the common literary origin, but, inversely, in the confluence of different literatures toward the same essential content. The miracle of the confluence is greater than the miracle of the unique author. Now the pole of this confluence is the ethical, which incontestably dominates this whole book.

Ph.N.: Would you go so far as to say that an ethical man could, at all times and places, give written or oral testimonies which could eventually constitute a Bible?

Or, that there could be a common Bible between men who belong to different traditions or who do not acknowledge themselves to be a part of any religious tradition?

E.L.: Yes, ethical truth is common. Bible reading, even if it is diverse, expresses in its diversity what each person brings to the Bible. The subjective condition of the reading is necessary to the reading of the prophetic. But one must certainly add to this the necessity of confrontation and dialogue, and consequently the whole problem of the call of tradition emerges, which is not an obedience but a hermeneutic.

Ph.N.: That goes without doubt for the reading of the same Bible by Jews and Christians. But my question went farther. I meant: if it is the testimony of the ethical which reveals the glory of the Infinite, and not a text containing a knowledge, what is the privilege of the Bible itself? Can one not read Plato as a Bible, or other great texts where humanity has acknowledged a testimony to the Infinite?

E.L.: In describing a moment ago — in passing — the human as a breakthrough that occurs in being and *puts into question* the proud independence of beings in their identity which it subjects to the *other*, I did not invoke the "fathomless" and utopian depths of "interiority." I have spoken of Scripture and the Book. I thought of their firmness which already tightens, hard as a verse, in all languages, before becoming letters traced by a stylet or quill. What one calls written in souls is at first written in books. Their status has always been too quickly made commonplace among the tools or cultural products of Nature or History. Even though their literature effects a rupture in being and does not come down to some unknown intimate voice, or to the normative abstraction of "values" that the world itself where we are cannot reduce to the objectivity of objects. I think that across all literature the human face speaks — or stammers, or gives itself a countenance, or struggles with its caricature. Despite the end of Europocentrism, disqualified by so many horrors, I believe in the eminence of the human face expressed in Greek Letters and in our own, which owe the Greeks everything. It is thanks to them that our history makes us ashamed. There is a participation in Holy Scripture in the national literatures, in Homer and Plato, in Racine and Victor Hugo, as in Pushkin, Dostoyevsky or Goethe, as of course in Tolstoy or in Agnon. But I am sure of the incomparable prophetic excellence of the Book of Books, which all the Letters of the world awaited or upon which they comment. The Holy Scriptures do not signify through the dogmatic tale of their supernatural or sacred origin, but through the expression of the face of the other man that they illuminate, before he gives himself a countenance or a pose. It is an expression as irrecusible as are imperious the worries of the everyday world of the historical beings that we are. The Holy Scriptures signify to me by all that they awakened in their readers in the course of centuries, and by all they received from exigeses and their transmission. They *command all the gravity of the ruptures* where in our being the good conscience of its being-there is put into question. Therein resides their very holiness, outside of every sacramental signification; a unique status, irreducible to that of the dreams of "beautiful souls," if one can still call status this wind of crisis — or this spirit — which blows and rends, despite the knots of History which retie themselves.

Ph.N.: The approach of the Infinite is thus essentially the same for every man. Nonetheless, only the particular religions give men consolations. The ethical exigency is universal, but consolation is a family affair?

E.L.: Religion in fact is not identical to philosophy, which does not necessarily bring the consolations which religion is able to give. Prophecy and ethics in no way exclude the consolations of religion; but I repeat again: a humanity which can do without these consolations perhaps may not be worthy of them.

Ph.N.: Let's speak about your most recent work. Nowadays you extend your meditation on responsibility for the Other by a meditation on responsibility for the Other's death. What should we understand by that?

E.L.: I think that in responsibility for the Other, one is, in the final analysis, responsible for the death of the other. Is not the rectitude of the other's look an exposure par excellence, an exposure unto death? The face in its uprightness is what is aimed at "point blank" by death. What is expressed as demand in it certainly signifies a call to *giving* and *serving* — or the commandment to giving and serving — but above this, and while including it, the order is to not let the Other alone, be it in the face of the inexorable. This is probably the foundation of sociality and of love without *eros*. The fear for the death of the other is certainly at the basis of the responsibility for him.

Such a fear is something other than fright. I think this notion of fear for the other man contrasts with the brilliant analyses Heidegger made of affectivity, sentiments, emotion, *Befindlichkeit*. Every emotion has, according to him, what he calls a double intentionality: it is an emotion *before* something and *for* something. Fear is fear *about* what is terrifying and always also fear *for* myself. Heidegger insists on the fact that in German verbs expressing emotions are always reflexive, as in French are the verbs to be moved, to be frightened, to be sad, etc. Anxiety, according to him, is an exceptional emotion wherein the *about* and the *for* coincide: anxiety *about* finitude is anxiety *for* my finitude and, in a certain sense, all emotion, because of this return to the self, goes back to anxiety. It seems to us that the fear for the other does not have this return to the self. Is it not in it that the emotion of fear of God regains its sense, disengaged from every reference to the idea of a jealous God?

Ph.N.: In what sense?

E.L.: Dis-inter-ested fear; timidity, shame . . . In any case, not fear of sanction.

Ph.N.: But if one fears for the Other and not for oneself, can one even live?

E.L.: This is in fact the question one must ultimately pose. Should I be dedicated to being? By being, by persisting in being, do I not kill?

Ph.N.: To be sure, now that the biological paradigm has become familiar to us, we know that every species lives at the expense of another, and that at the interior of each species every individual replaces another. One cannot live without killing.

E.L.: In society such as it functions one cannot live without killing, or at least without taking the preliminary steps for the death of someone. Consequently, the important question of the meaning of being is not: why is there something rather than nothing — the Leibnizian question so much commented upon by Heidegger — but: do I not kill by being?

Ph.N.: Even though, from this acknowledgement that one cannot live without murder, or at least without struggle, others draw the conclusion that it is necessary in fact to kill, and that violence serves life and rules evolution, you refuse this answer?

E.L.: The explosion of the human in being, the breakthrough of being about which I have spoken in the course of these interviews, the crisis of being, the otherwise than being, are indeed marked by the fact that what is most natural becomes the most problematic. Do I have the right to be? Is being in the world not taking the place of someone? The naive and natural perseverance in being is put into question!

Ph.N.: In an epigraph to *Otherwise than Being* you cite a sentence of Pascal: "This is my place in the sun. That is how the usurpation of the whole world began", and "They have used concupiscence as best they could for the general good. But it is only pretense, and a false image of charity. For at bottom it is only hatred."[2]

However, if one agrees with you that this question is the ultimate question, or first, of metaphysics, how are you committed to your own answer? Will you go so far as to say that you do not have the right to live?

E.L.: In no way do I want to teach that suicide follows from the love of the neighbor and the truly

2. Pascal, *Pensées*; Brunschvicg 295 and 451/LaFuma 112 and 404.

human life. I mean to say that a truly human life cannot remain life *satis*-fied in its equality to being, a life of quietude, that it is awakened by the other, that is to say, it is always getting sobered up, that being is never — contrary to what so many reassuring traditions say — its own reason for being, that the famous *conatus essendi* is not the source of all right and all meaning.

Major Works of
Emmanuel Levinas[1]

Théorie de l'intuition dans la phénoménologie de Husserl (Paris:
Vrin, 1930, 1963, 1970).
 The Theory of Intuition in Husserl's Phenomenology, transl.
 by André Orianne (Evanston, Illinois: Northwest-
 ern, 1973).
Le temps et l'autre, in J. Wahl, *Le Choix, Le Monde, L'Existence*
(Grenoble-Paris: Arthaud, 1947) pp. 125-196.
 Le Temps et l'Autre (Montpellier: Fata Morgana, 1979).
De l'existent à l'existence (Paris: Vrin, 1947).
 Existence and Existents, transl. by Alphonso Lingis
 (The Hague: Nijhoff, 1978).
En découvrant l'existence avec Husserl et Heidegger (Paris: Vrin,
 1949; 2nd ed., 1967, 1974).
Totalité et Infini (La Haye, Nijhoff, 1961, 1965, 1968, 1971,
 1974).
 Totality and Infinity, transl. by Alphonso Lingis (The

---

1. The most complete bibliography of Levinas' published
 works, as well as secondary publications (to 1981), is *Emmanuel Levinas* by Roger Burggraeve, issued in 1982 by the
 Center for Metaphysics and Philosophy of God, Institute of
 Philosophy, Kardinaal Mercierplein 2, 3000 Leuven, Belgium.

Hague: Nijhoff, 1969); (Pittsburgh: Duquesne, 1969, 1979).

Difficile liberté (Paris: Albin Michel, 1963).

Quatre lectures talmudiques (Paris: Minuit, 1968).

Humanisme de 'lAutre homme (Montpellier: Fata Morgana, 1972).

Autrement qu'être, ou au-delà de l'essence (La Haye, Nijhoff, 1974). *Otherwise than Being or Beyond Essence*, transl. by Alphonso Lingis (The Hague: Nijhoff, 1981).

Sur Maurice Blanchot (Montpellier: Fata Morgana, 1975).

Noms propres (Montpellier: Fata Morgana, 1975).

Du sacré au Saint (Paris: Minuit, 1977).

L'Au-delà du verset (Paris: Minuit, 1982).

De Dieu qui vient à l'idée (Paris: Vrin, 1982).

Index of Names

Agnon, S. J., 117
Amos, 113

Bergson, Henri, 26-28, 38, 40
Blanchot, Maurice, 49, 50
Blondel, Charles, 25

Carteron, Henri, 25
Claudel, Paul, 110

Descartes, René, 26, 60, 77, 91, 92, 109
Dostoyevsky, Fyodor, 22, 98, 101
Durkheim, Emile, 26, 27

Gandhi, M. K., 13
Goethe, Johann Wolgang von, 117
Gogol, Nikolay, 22

Halbwachs, Maurice, 25, 26
Hegel, George Wilhelm Friedrich, 26, 37, 43, 76, 78
Heidegger, Martin 1-6, 27, 31, 37-44, 47, 52, 58, 90, 95, 119, 121

Hölderlin, J. C. F., 42
Homer, 117
Hugo, Victor, 117
Husserl, Edmund, 28-33, 37-39, 42, 47, 61, 90

Kant, Immanuel, 22, 26, 37
Kafka, F., 15

Leibniz, Gottfried, 78
Lermontov, Mikhail, 22

Marx, Karl, 43
Merleau-Ponty, Maurice, 32, 56

Nietzsche, 3, 4, 6

Pascal, 121
Peiffer, Gabrielle, 29
Plato, vii, 22, 26, 37, 72, 116, 117
Pradines, Marice, 25
Pushkin, Alexander, 22, 117

Racine, Jean, 117
Rosenzweig, Franz, 75, 76

Sartre, Jean-Paul, 43, 56
Shakespeare, 22
Socrates, 5, 12, 91

Tolstoy, Leo, 22, 117
Turgenev, Ivan, 22

Van Breda, H. L., 33

Wahl, Jean, 55, 70